MY LITTLE BOOK OF HAPPINESS
Positive Affirmations for Children

Words by
Ruth Blackburn

Illustrations by
Arzu Dever

Design copyright © Little Wise Things 2020
Illustrations copyright © Arzu H. Dever 2020

All rights reserved.

No part of this book may be reproduced, stored or distributed by any means including photocopying, without the prior written permission of the copyright owner, except in the use of quotations for critical reviews or educational references.

First paperback edition August 2020

Book design by Ruth H. Blackburn and
           Arzu H. Dever

Written by Ruth H. Blackburn
Illustrated by Arzu H. Dever

ISBN 978-1-5272-6732-9 (paperback)

Published by Little Wise Things
www.littlewisethings.co.uk

Dedicated to our daughters **Sia**, **Evie** and **Duru**

forever our inspiration...

...and to every child around the world, keep smiling and believe in yourself.
(You're doing great!)

How to use this book

① Find a mirror.

② Look at your wonderful face and smile.

③ Read each page in a strong, clear voice.

④ Believe in yourself. You are AMAZING!

My name is

....

It's good to be me!

I am bright like a Shining Star.

I have good ideas and my voice is important.

  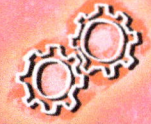

$8 \times 2 = 16$

I can do difficult tasks.

$3 \times 3 = 9$

$5 \times 3 = 15$

MISTAKES

Mistakes help me to learn.

I am proud of myself.

I am kind to myself and to others.

I make good choices.

I feel better when I talk about my feelings.

Now...

Keep looking in the mirror and SMILE until your eyes twinkle!

www.ingramcontent.com/pod-product-compliance
Lightning Source LLC
Chambersburg PA
CBHW061131070526
44584CB00033B/4297